BEING HAPPIER

Praise For Stella's Transformational Coaching Program "THE PASSPORT"

Dear Stella,

Many joyful things have happened I believe because I committed to me, you, and your program.

Tasks that have sat for years were suddenly easy to complete, more business has flowed into my life. Didn't matter how imperfectly or maybe even because I did not color inside the lines. Progress not perfection!

So you don't ever have to wonder if I will be on the call. I will be there looking forward to the new each of us has collectively come to be.

One last thing. Don't let my snarky side or anyone else's stop you from calling. Your willingness to call even though I didn't call, meant the world to me.

Your kindness, generosity and courage rock my world. So keep calling us when you're inspired. You may not know that it is the seed needed for transformation. <3

All my heart,
Nancy W

Praise For Stella's "Lasting Happiness" Presentation

Stella is awesome at helping improve…and we all have room for improvement. Garry A.

Mind opening on Change. Groundbreaking event. Jeff B.

Entertaining. Thought provoking. Soul searching. Roy E.

I learned why embracing change and practicing gratitude can help me be happy. Niki G.

I can't imagine anyone that couldn't learn and enjoy Stella's presentation. Wonderful experience. Thank you "Happy" you are a gift to all of us. Karin M.

Stella glows. Happiness is the biggest gift and Stella is a "Happiness Generator" Frannie S.

Learning about the stages of change helped me understand where stand and what step to take next. Thank you Stella. Bill H.

Listening to Stella's information about change and happiness shifted my thinking to move forward in a positive way. Marty G.

Stay positive, break the chains, be happy. Sandra E.

Don't miss the next one! Alan H.

Other STELLA NOTES BOOKS

- ❖ In The Sea of Love
- ❖ Law of Attraction
- ❖ Imagine
- ❖ Dreams Come True
- ❖ Being Happier
- ❖ Inspired
- ❖ No Worries
- ❖ Happy by Habit
- ❖ How To Say No
- ❖ Stuck No More
- ❖ Love Thyself
- ❖ Mindfully Yours
- ❖ Find Your Purpose

Every Month we add new titles in our Happiness Library filled with tips and tools to make your journey a Fun One! Be sure to check them out!

This book is being given to

_____

Because I care about you and your happiness

With Love,

_____

BEING HAPPIER

Living The Life You Love

STELLA FRANCES

Happiness Coach & Success Trainer

Alpha ★ Aster Press

Copyright © 2019 by Stella Frances

All rights reserved. Printed in the United States of America.
This book or any portion thereof may not be reproduced or used in any manner whatsoever without the express written permission of the publisher except for the use of brief quotations in critical articles and reviews.
For information address: Alpha Aster Press, 103 S Us Hwy One, Ste F-5, Jupiter, FL, 33477

First Printing: 2019

ISBN 978-0-359-53567-5

Alpha★Aster Press

Cover design: ZettaKarmas.com
Photos of Stella: WoodstockStudio.com

Ordering Information: Special discounts are available on quantity purchases by corporations, associations, educators, and others. For details, contact the publisher at the above listed address.

U.S. trade bookstores and wholesalers, contact Alpha★Aster Press sales@alphaaster.com

This book is dedicated to You:

Wishing you the best of success on your quest to discovering your truth…

Stella Frances

---

*Very little is needed to make a happy life;
it is all within yourself, in your way of thinking.*

MARCUS AURELIUS

CONTENTS

Preface Iii

Introduction By Stella Frances Vii

ACT I: INFORMATIVE GUIDEBOOK 1

Introduction 3

« Chapter One » Building Your Bridge... 5

« Chapter Two » Live In The Now 13

« Chapter Three » Choose Conscious Living 19

« Chapter Four » Take Right Action.. 31

« Chapter Five » The Checklist.................................... 39

ACT II: EMPOWERING WORKBOOK.. 45

« Chapter Six » Happier Through Reflection................................ 47

ACT III: KEY FACTS.. 59

« Chapter Seven » Secrets To Being Happier 61

NOTES AT A GLANCE 69

ACT IV: Happiness Builders... 77

« Chapter Eight » Tools-To-Use 79

Words Of Wisdom 81

Pearls Of Kindness 85

Relaxing Mandalas... 89

IN CLOSING: Bonus Material - A Gift For You... 95

AFTERWORD: Resource Guide For Living A Happier Life 99

Acknowledgments

I acknowledge with heartfelt happiness and gratitude:

My clients and students for their encouragement to spread the word about true happiness through the Stella Notes.

My participants to my seminars and presentations who have shown their support for my work and who continue to be an inspiration to me.

My mentors and teachers who shared their knowledge and wisdom with me, while they believed in my wildest dream and breakthrough goal: To spread happiness around the globe!

Everyone who makes the effort to bring a smile to the world, even on the days the sun's hiding behind the clouds.

My awesome friends, amazing family, and the best sister in the whole wide world who surround me with unconditional love, smiles, and fun times.

Knowing yourself is the beginning of all wisdom.
ARISTOTLE

"I Believe We Were Born To Be Happy"

Mentor, Coach, Speaker, Creator of Stella-Notes

Hi and thank you for checking out this publication. Stella Frances, here, founder of Elevated Awareness, on a mission to empower you.

My goal is to add more value to your world than you ever thought possible by giving you tools you can use to live a great life.

Having trained with Jack Canfield, America's #1 Success Coach and Co-Author of "Chicken Soup for the Soul", and as a certified DreamBuilder Coach, I am known to deliver innovative and high-quality personal development training with proven results that have changed many lives.

I help people like you dream big and back it up with daily actions to create measurable results. That's because I care deeply about you and I am committed to not only get you results but make learning irresistibly fun.

Through my products, seminars, and programs you'll learn practical wisdom and how to apply it to your everyday life. Through the Stella Notes, I want to encourage you and inspire you to take charge of your happiness and success by boosting your life and business skills, dropping excuses and adding massive amounts of fun into your every day.

Make the most of the Stella Notes by completing the exercises, practicing daily affirmation, and building new habits that will contribute to taking your happiness and wellbeing to the next level. Much Love. Stella

THE GREATEST GIFT: YOUR OWN PERSONAL DEVELOPMENT

The greatest gift you can give somebody is your own personal development.

I used to say, "If you will take care of me, I will take care of you."

Now I say, "I will take care of me for you, if you will take care of you for me."

—Jim Rohn

The Stella Notes is all about personal development for everyone, within the context of self-discovery & transformation. Personal development is the ongoing, lifelong process of learning, knowing and understanding who we are, why we're here and what work we have come to do in our lifetime, what our gifts and abilities are, and how to build them up, so that we can live up to our highest potential.

If you find yourself in a situation that needs to change. If you have reached a plateau wondering what's next, look at the "man/woman in the mirror" and decide to make a change by changing your ways. the *Stella Notes* gives you winning ways to successfully do so.

CLUB ★ HAPPY

Know thyself.
SOCRATES

The success that followed the launching of the Stella Notes led me to the next step which was to create a loving, caring, physical or virtual space, where we get to connect, share ideas, and support each other. And so, the Club was born!

"Club-Happy" is not your ordinary book club. Consider it your social group, your support group, your mastermind group, your cheerleader group. Once a week we get together in-person or on a call to connect by brainstorming new ideas, solving problems, learning from each other and growing together.

Fact of life is that we need each other to grow and evolve, especially when we decide to make a change. Our motto at the Club-Happy is simple. We come together with the aim to live better lives by finding and implementing empowering solutions to the problems we are experiencing in our personal and professional lives. The intention of Club-Happy is to help each other grow and expand by implementing the practices, tools, and strategies that are included in the Stella Notes books.

Be Part Of An Empowering Group Of People

Having 2,000 friends on Facebook may be great but personal connections are much more powerful. Club-Happy is about building great relationships personal and professional, as we get together and connect by sharing knowledge and helping each other grow.

As a member of Club-Happy you are an important part of a conscious community that shares the same vision. The vision of attaining and maintaining true happiness. A peaceful, balanced, and harmonious way of being.

There are so many reasons why join Club-Happy. Every in-person meeting or call is well structured with clear boundaries and expectations, runs based on a mutually agreed upon agenda to help us stay on track as we share evenly.

Why Join CLUB* HAPPY:

1. To create deep, lasting connections with like-minded people.
2. To clear confusion and gain focus and clarity on your vision.
3. To be courageous, advantageous and spontaneous.
4. To become the person, you know you can be.
5. To create a clear vision and an action plan.
6. To socialize and be part of a fun group.
7. To think bigger and more creatively.
8. To be accountable.
9. To support others.
10. To be supported.
11. To be happier.
12. To be You.

I invite you to join me today and start enjoying the tremendous benefits of being part of Club-Happy. Visit https://stellafrances.com/clubhappy/ for more information or reach out with your questions, at Happier@StellaFrances.com

INTRODUCTION BY STELLA FRANCES
Suggestions To My Readers

A very warm welcome to this reading experience. My intention for creating the Stella Notes, series of practical books, is very specific. I want to help you harness your inner-power, connect with your truth, and create a life that is in harmony with your soul. And in return I promise, you will get to deep lasting happiness, for the only place to find your true happy is within you.

The Stella Notes will help you learn new ways of bringing positive change into your life in the most effective winning ways with the least amount of effort. Originally, I created the *Stella Notes,* with a specific audience in the mind of my heart. The people who have no time to read and the people who are not fans of reading. **My sister gave me the idea.** Knowledge is power, but reading is not her favorite past time.

As an artist, my sister Zetta, loves to paint. Often, I'd hear her say, *"If there was a book for non-readers, I would read it."* By that she meant, a few pages, clear language easy to read, helpful to the point useful material and of course pictures. Being an avid reader myself I didn't want her to miss out on knowledge and so here we are.

How To Use The Stella Notes Books

The Stella Notes is a series of books structured to make reading and absorption of the material real easy. The information is presented in four sections. Each section is called **ACT.** Here's what you will find in every Stella Notes book:

❖ **ACT I:** Guidebook: Theory of Concept.

❖ **ACT II:** Workbook: Self-Reflection on the Concept.

❖ **ACT III:** Key Facts: Additional Information.

❖ **ACT IV:** Mindful and Practical Tools-to-Use.

You can read the guidebook in *ACT I* at one seating or in small bits, however it suits you. Answer the questions in the workbook as presented in *ACT II* at your pace. Here, you can write down the answers in your book or get a notebook and start jotting them down there. In *ACT III* **Key Facts** you will find additional information about the main subject.

While in *ACT IV* you will be pleasantly surprised by a beautiful collection of words of wisdom, pearls of kindness in the form of heartfelt affirmations, and magnificent mandalas to help you stay in the moment, find inner peace and express your inner-artist. The pearls of kindness are beautiful positive statements designed to help you build new empowering beliefs through repetition. The words of wisdom I bring to you, were spoken by some of the most powerful and advanced thinkers in our world. Listen to the echo of their voices and use their valuable knowledge in your moment-to-moment life.

In the Afterword section, under resources you will find tools you can use to build the above ideas and they are all totally **FREE**. This is my way of saying Thank You. *Go to the website StellaFrances.com/resources and download them there.* Use the *Gratitude Journal* to record you wins and gifts of the day. Use the *Get Unstuck Tool* for days when you feel just a tad stuck…we all go there and need this tool. Same with the *Priority Finder Tool.*

Who doesn't get stressed or overwhelmed with the complexities of our lives? The ***Daily Success Habits*** will help you with just that. Create new success habits. Finally, the ***5-Day Grow-Expand-Thrive Mini Course*** will help you exhilarate towards your new life. The life of your choice.

Why Read The Stella Notes Books? Because You Will Learn New, Winning Ways Of Thinking…Guarantee!

The practice of planting high quality seedlings of new positive, powerful, constructive thoughts in our minds creates our ideal results. I've been practicing and experimenting this truth for the past 20 years. I know it works.

Remember this. To change your LifeStyle, you must first change your ThoughtStyle. Opening up to the thoughts of great thinkers is one sure way to get inspired and start thinking different thoughts. Makes sense? Albert Einstein defined insanity as the act of trying to solve a problem with the same thinking that created it.

At first, it may seem or even feel a little strange but stay with it. Give it time, let it flourish. You will be amazed at what you will harvest.

Happiness is the meaning and the purpose of life, the whole aim and end of human existence. ARISTOTLE

Are You Willing To Believe In Yourself?

Finally, a word of caution. As with anything worth having in life it takes time, commitment and dedication. It takes effort to create something worth having.

❖ *What's worth more than, living a life you totally love living?*

❖ *What's worth more than, being happy from within?*

❖ *What's worth more than, having found meaning in your life?*

So, go ahead dare to design your life, find meaning and live it the way you want, for you know best how to find what you're looking for. And as you do, practice self-love through kindness and forgiveness towards yourself. Be patient with you.

Be the light of love in your life. Give yourself the best love you can give yourself. <u>**BELIEVE IN YOU**</u>. **And when you do, you will be amazed as you discover who you truly are and what you can create when you release the brakes of yesterday.**

Read the Stella Notes, Solutions from the Soul, any way you like. Cover to cover, one paragraph, one quote, one affirmation at a time. Keep your book by your side, make it your constant companion. It is designed in such way that however you use it you will feel inspired to move forward from where you are.

Whether you read one page, one sentence or just run the questions you will start seeing changes and eventually results in your life. You will find yourself be more motivated, more engaged, more curious, more alive and above all happier.

"Magically?" You may ask.

Well, life is magical and so are you. Once you start tapping into your super powers there will be no stopping. You have in your procession an amazing tool, an extraordinary component. That is your brain. And you are given unlimited potential. Put them to work with the information I will be sharing with you through the Stella Notes books and you will be well on your way to creating pure and lasting happiness and unstoppably so.

You are brave. Choose to leave behind the voice of fear and doubt and you will be amazed at what you will create. Courage is not the absence of fear. Courage is facing fear.

The Stella Notes books bring you unique concepts that focus on mindset, contribute to your personal growth, and provide you with tools you can use and strategies to implement that will help you change your thoughts and therefore your world.

Let's begin!

With Love and Gratitude,
XO Stella

P.S. If you know it's time to bring radical change into your life and need support, reach out and contact me through the website. I am here to help.

ACT I:

INFORMATIVE GUIDEBOOK

knowledge:
the pathway to
happiness & success

The primary cause of
unhappiness is
never the situation but
your thoughts about it.
Eckhart Tolle

Being Happier
Living The Life You Love

Introduction

Are you thirsting for a better, bigger, more meaningful life? The Being "Happier -Living The Life You Love" book is your toolkit to building your bridge from the life you have now to the one your heart is yearning for.

The information in this book will help you find success in different areas of your life, including your relationships, finances, faith, health, work, and more. You'll find specific action steps you can take, to live your IDEAL life. Start by reading the guidebook and as you go through it, reflect on the lessons and apply them to your own life. Next, complete the empowering self-reflection workbook to initiate the changes in any area of your life you wish to strengthen. The guidebook explains how to correctly use this for the best effect.

Lastly, use the checklist and notes as reminders to incorporate each strategy into your daily routine.

I ask that you take the time to make the most of this package and take advantage of the life-altering strategies. You'll soon enjoy the rewards of living a deeply fulfilling life.

Investing in yourself is the best investment you will ever make. It will not only improve your life, it will improve the lives of all those around you.
ROBIN SHARMA

« Chapter One »

BUILDING YOUR BRIDGE

ARE YOU LONGING for a more meaningful, happier life, filled with abundance in every area? Love, Health, Fun, Finance, and Time Freedom?

No matter where in life you are or what is going on, the life you desire is possible, if you put your mind to it.

You might have heard the axiom, "If you keep doing what you've been doing, you'll keep getting what you've got." In order for things to change, you need to do something differently.

Doing things differently starts with a change in your thoughts. When you change your thinking, you automatically change your actions to be in alignment with your new thoughts and attitudes.

But how do you think differently to attract what you desire? Do you just wish for it really hard and then assume that you'll do the right thing? No. Not at all. In fact, wishing too hard can push it farther and farther away from you. I'll explain why in this book.

On the contrary, there are tangible things you can do every day to change your thoughts and your life.

Let's begin.

When You Demonstrate The Life You Want, You'll Attract It Back Toward You.

Granted, you can't just leap from your life into your dream life in a single step, but you can build the bridge that enables you to cross over in the shortest possible time.

Start out with some conscious actions and follow through consistently every day. These actions become habits and help you ingrain new thoughts and attitudes into your subconscious mind.

These new thoughts and attitudes are the ones that will attract your dream life. They make up the mindset that requires you to act in accordance with the life you want.

❖ Do you desire financial freedom?

- Could your relationships use some more passion?
- What about your physical self – are you satisfied with your body?
- Do you feel joy and happiness in your life? Do you want more?

You can make all these things happen. All it takes is a commitment to bring this abundance into your life and the follow-up actions to make it a reality.

This book will guide you through **specific action steps** you can take to live the life you love. Engage in these actions every day, and begin to discover the life of harmony, joy and happiness you've always wanted.

YOUR PERCEPTION IS YOUR REALITY

Is your glass half full or half empty?

How you perceive the events in your life – both big and small – not only shows your underlying mindset about your life, but also plays the most important role in whether you reach your goals.

Let's use the glass to demonstrate this concept. Imagine the glass has tasty lemonade in it, and you really like lemonade. What are your thoughts when you see it?

If you're optimistic, of course you see it as half full. You may have thoughts like these:

- "Oh, boy. I've got some delicious lemonade to quench my thirst."

Employ your time in improving yourself by other men's writings so that you shall come easily by what others have labored hard for.
Socrates

- ❖ As you reach for the glass, you feel anticipation and gratitude for this good and tasty drink.
- ❖ Your thoughts are happily focused on what you have in this moment, not on what you lack.

The simple joy of some nice, cool lemonade and the good feelings that go along with it cause your brain to send out energy that vibrates in harmony with good things and **attracts more good things back to you.**

Now look at what happens when you're a pessimist and see the glass as half empty. Your thoughts may be closer to these:

- ❖ "Oh, great (sarcastically). I'm so thirsty and all I've got is half a glass of lemonade."
- ❖ As you reach for the glass, you feel dissatisfaction. You wish you had more.
- ❖ Your thoughts are on what you lack.

Not only do you miss out on any enjoyment from the lemonade, but your mind sends out energy that vibrates in harmony with dissatisfaction and lack. What do you think you'll attract back to you? More things to be unhappy about and more lack.

This also explains why wishing for something too hard can push it away from you forever. **When you're wishing for something you don't have, you're focusing on your lack of it.** Focusing on your lack of it only attracts more lack of it back to you.

This simple glass of lemonade shows how your perception is your reality. **Two different people can have two totally different experiences from the same circumstance.** One person's experience adds to the happiness of a joyful life and the other's adds more problems to their unsatisfying existence. It also explains why some people can make lemonade (and enjoy it) when life hands them lemons, while some just can't.

When you apply this lesson to your own life, what do you find? Are you attracting good things or more lack? Could you use some ways to change your mindset?

11 BEING **HAPPIER**

Happiness is part of who we are.
Joy is the feeling.
Tony DeLiso

12 STELLA FRANCES

« Chapter Two »

LIVE IN THE NOW

IT'S BEEN SAID, *"the fastest way to get where you want to be, is to be happy with where you are."* This seems almost contradictory, but, in fact, it reveals a great truth.

The more "good vibrations" you send out, the more good things you attract back to you to be happy about. One of the best ways to be sending out good vibrations consistently is to live in the moment.

What does this mean? It means that you remain in the now – not yesterday or tomorrow. You treat each moment as the precious thing that it is and enjoy it to its fullest. You immerse yourself fully in the moment.

Living In The Moment Can Also:

- ✓ Reduce stress
- ✓ Relieve worry about the future
- ✓ Eliminate anguish about the past
- ✓ Enable you to brush away distractions and focus on your task at hand
- ✓ Bring more passion to your relationships
- ✓ Allow to you leap toward achieving your goals faster than you ever thought possible
- ✓ Let you enjoy the peace, happiness, and contentment of a fulfilling life

Next, I present you six action steps you can take to help you live in the moment:

Action Step #1:
Watch The Movie "The Peaceful Warrior"

This movie will bring you a great understanding about living in the moment. It's based on events in the life of champion gymnast Dan Millman.

After a tragic accident paralyzes him, his doctors say he'll never walk again. With the help of his mentor who teaches him to live in the moment, Dan not only walks, but competes as a world champion gymnast once again. It's a true story and reveals exceptionally well how living in the moment can truly change your life for the better. As his mentor teaches him the philosophy and techniques, so, too, will you learn.

Action Step #2:
Take Time To Stop And Smell The Roses

This applies not only to enjoying the simple, good things in life, but it also applies to literally taking the time to notice what's around you so you can take pleasure from what your senses bring you.

- ❖ Notice the physical world around you.
- ❖ Cherish its beauty.

Revel in the majesty of the sunset, the wonderful aroma of the roses, the delicious taste of good food, the pleasing harmony of music, and the soft touch of a loved one.

Action Step #3:
Avoid Total Focus On Your Goals

Never get so caught up in pursuing your goals that you cease to enjoy the present. **Your life is your journey.** Enjoy what you've got when you've got it. Otherwise, you might wake up some day and realize that you missed living altogether.

Action Step #4:
Make The Most Of Each Moment

Realize that every moment of your life is a gift. Get all the good out of it that you can. If you make a mistake, learn something from that moment and move on.

Action Step #5:
Look For The Silver Lining

Practice finding the good, even when things don't go as expected. Many times, you can even get something better than you had planned, if you just open your mind to the possibilities that there is something good to be discovered.

Action Step #6:
Eliminate Time Spent Waiting

Avoid just sitting around and waiting for things to happen. Take advantage of your time by making it productive. Use it to listen to motivational audio books, share delightful insights with the people next to you, plan your day, or read something that educates, inspires, or relaxes you.

There's a Zimbabwe proverb that says, "If you can walk, you can dance. If you can talk, you can sing." Like the proverb, living in the moment lets you live with excitement instead of mediocre. Living in the now gives you a reason to dance instead of walk and sing instead of talk.

Living in the moment takes some practice, but the more you do it, the easier it gets. Practice this every day, and soon it will become a habit that changes your mindset and helps you live a life full of passion, joy, and happiness.

ACTION NOTES

LIVE IN THE NOW

1. Watch: "The Peaceful Warrior"
2. Make time to smell the roses
3. Avoid total focus on your goals
4. Make the most of every minute
5. Look For The Silver Lining
6. Eliminate Time Spent Waiting

Knowing others is intelligence;
knowing yourself is true wisdom.
Mastering others is strength;
mastering yourself is true power.
Lao Tzu

« Chapter Three »

CHOOSE CONSCIOUS LIVING

CONSCIOUS LIVING, JUST like living in the moment, involves being aware of what's around you and choosing to make the most of what you've got, but it takes things a step further. Conscious living brings in the added factor of making certain choices that can bring you the life you desire.

Conscious living is *living on purpose.* You choose how you want to live your life and then live that way.

The following four strategies for living consciously will help bring your goals to fruition:

Strategy #1
Set Priorities In Your Life

Decide what's most important to you and live according to these priorities. Having clear priorities makes it easier for you to make decisions about your time, money and other important items that matter to you.

Strategy #2
Choose To Have An Optimistic Attitude

As we've already seen, this conscious living choice can have an enormous impact on your life.

Each morning when you wake up, tell yourself that this day will be your best day ever. Helen Keller once said, *"Life is either a daring adventure or nothing."* We don't know ahead of time all the things the day will bring, so look forward to it with anticipation as an exciting adventure and live your day accordingly.

Strategy #3
Simplify Your Lifestyle

Put the things into your life that you want there, according to your priorities, and eliminate the things that merely serve to clutter it up and cause confusion and stress.

Events and activities that eat up your time and take away from your family time are a good example of things you can eliminate from your life. A hectic lifestyle can be a major cause of distractions and stress.

Will it really matter if you decline a couple of parties or miss a PTA meeting here and there? Once you get used to putting only those things in your schedule that you feel are a priority, you'll wonder why you didn't learn to say *No* sooner.

Is your house or office space cluttered? Once again, **eliminate what you don't want or need.** Take a weekend to go through everything in your house, organize what you want to keep, and give away what you no longer have a use for.

Enjoy dinner at home with the family. Use this time to catch up with each other, share your day and show your love and support. Make this time a priority and you'll soon see some of your family stressors melt away as you build stronger relationships that will last a lifetime.

Strategy #4
Live According To Your Principles

Remember, when you live consciously, you're choosing your life.

Let your principles guide you in making your priorities and decisions. Above all, get clear on your values, standards, and principles so you can be true to yourself.

Living consciously gives you a chance to start demonstrating the life you desire. You may not have as much money as you'd like, or you might want to lose some weight, or you may be seeking your soul mate, but following these strategies puts everything in motion.

With conscious living, your thought processes are emitting energy harmonious with attracting what you want and your actions are in accordance with them.

Rather than spending your time focusing on what is lacking, you spend your time and energies choosing your life and living it to the fullest, thus attracting more good things in return.

STRATEGY NOTES

CHOOSE CONSCIOUS LIVING

1. Set Priorities In Your Life
2. Adapt An Optimistic Attitude
3. Simplify Your Lifestyle
4. Honor Your Principles

I would maintain that thanks are the highest form of thought, and that gratitude is happiness doubled by wonder.
Gilbert K. Chesterton

CHOOSE GRATITUDE

How gratitude can attract what you want. Gratitude plays a big part in attracting your dream life. **Feeling thankful for your blessings attracts more things for you to be thankful for.** Even if what you've got isn't much, it can be increased a hundred-fold by being thankful for it.

In addition, when you show your gratitude to others for something, they've done for you, they're more inclined to do even more. Gratitude strengthens the bonds of friendship and increases the loyalty of business associates.

The following winning ways will help you express your gratitude on a daily basis and reap the benefits:

Winning Way #1
Show Your Appreciation

Tell others when they make you happy The need to feel appreciated is one of our basic human needs. Fulfill that need and share the love. A simple "Thank you" can make their day.

Your parents and children love to know when they've made you happy. Make it a habit to thank them often.

Letting your spouse know how much you appreciate them and all they do, will strengthen your relationship even more. It can also start a cycle of you both doing nice things for each other, because you know how much the other one appreciates it.

Your friends also like to know that they bring value to your life. Every so often, do something special to show your gratitude.

Co-workers, business associates, and clients also like to know they're appreciated. When they do something for you, be sure to say "Thank you" and let them know how much it means to you. Offer to reciprocate by helping them when they need it, too.

Remember to thank the clerk at the bank, the customer service rep who went out of their way to solve your problem, or the store employee who helped you find what you were looking for.

The more you make it a point to thank those who make your life better, the more you find to be thankful for. After all, you don't want to be taking things for granted.

Winning Way #2
Keep A Gratitude Journal

At the end of each day, reflect on all that is good and write it down in your journal. Reading about all the things you're thankful for can also lift your spirits and motivate you.

Winning Way #3
Give Thanks

When you awake, give thanks for the day ahead and all its wonderful possibilities. Before you fall asleep at night, give thanks for the day you just had.

Feeling gratitude every day keeps the good things coming. **Nothing's too small to be thankful for.** If you find a penny on the ground, be grateful for the gift. Even if you desire greater wealth, be thankful for the paycheck you just got.

Gratitude helps you feel fulfilled with your life and it sends out energy with those good vibrations.

Winning Way
Over-Deliver On Your Promises

Another technique that helps you attract the life you desire is to give more than is expected. When you give more to others (as opposed to taking more), you're sending out energy that attracts good things back to you.

Consistently over-delivering on your promises suggests a mindset of excellence and abundance. Aren't these some of the important qualities included in your dream life?

When you generously give more than you promise, you make others happy. You also feel good about yourself, which strengthens your self-esteem and self-confidence. These are the very traits that you see in anyone who is successful.

So by increasing these qualities and traits within yourself, you're setting yourself up for success in achieving your life's desires.

NOTES: WINNING WAYS

CHOOSE GRATITUDE

1. Show Your Appreciation
2. Keep A Gratitude Journal
3. Give Thanks
4. Over-Deliver On Your Promises

When one door of happiness closes, another opens -but often we look so long at the closed door that we don't see the one that has been opened for us.
Helen Keller

30 STELLA FRANCES

« Chapter Four »

TAKE RIGHT ACTION

T**URN YOUR DREAMS** into your reality. If you want anything to happen in your life, you need to take action. When you set a goal, you got to take some form of action to accomplish it. If there's something you are unhappy with, don't put up with it "just because" that's the way it is – you can do something about it.

You'll find that when you strive to become action-oriented, more things go your way quicker than ever before.

One reason for this is that taking action keeps you from sitting around just wishing for more, while you focus on whatever you're missing in your life. After all, if you believe it's missing, then that's just the way it will stay – missing.

Focus, instead, on making a plan and implementing it. As you work to achieve your goals, your focus will shift on what you can do.

Create An Action Plan You Know You Can Accomplish

Setting yourself up for success with your action plan is important. Otherwise, you might feel as if you're just spinning your wheels. For example, if you set goals that are unreachable, you're quite likely to give up before you ever really get started.

How can you set yourself up for success with your action plan?

Use these tips to **set S.M.A.R.T. goals** that will bring you the success you desire:

1. SPECIFIC. State exactly what it is you want to accomplish. Rather than saying you want to make more money, state how much more, for example, $12,000 per year.

2. MEASURABLE. You must be able to measure your goal so you know when you've accomplished it and can move on to your next goal. The goal in the above example is measurable because it's a real number to work towards.

3. ATTAINABLE. Divide your goal into attainable mini-goals that you can accomplish in a short period of time. If you desire $12,000 more per year, you can divide it into $1,000 per month, or $250 per week.

4. REACHABLE. Is your goal reachable for you? Do you have some way you can reach that $250 per week goal?

If not, then rethink your goal. Perhaps you first need to take action on implementing another income stream or you need to go to school to get additional skills or credentials in your current job before you can progress to the $250 per week goal.

5. TIMELY. Set a timeline and a specific date in which all steps will be completed. This will, of course, depend on your goal. If you need to take a 6-month course to further your education or skills, then that first goal will end in 6 months.

Once you're sure you've created a plan you know you can accomplish, you've already set yourself up for success. All that's required now is that you follow your plan.

Implementing Your Action Plan

In order to follow through with your plan, there are a few more strategies you can implement to make it a success:

1. Make The First Steps Easy And Quick. Put easy tasks at the beginning so you'll be able to jump right in and get started quickly. This will give you confidence and motivate you to keep going.

2. Reward Yourself For Each Accomplishment. No matter how small your micro-goals are, pat yourself on the back each time you achieve one of them.

Take pride in your achievements and enjoy your success. Remember, this sends out energies that will bring back more things to be proud about.

Treat yourself to a little reward for the small goals and a bigger one for completing major milestones. This gives you some immediate gratification and something to look forward to with each step.

3. Change Your Plan If Necessary. If you find your plan isn't working for you, it's much better to alter your mini-goals to something that you can accomplish than to keep failing at achieving them. Remember, you want to set yourself up for success.

Taking action is a given. Taking the right actions can bring your IDEAL outcome to you a lot faster. This is why it's so important to develop a mindset and attitude that encourages you to take direct actions toward success.

MIND TOOLS TO CHANGE YOUR LIFE

To transform your mindset into one which attracts what you want, it's necessary to incorporate your desired thoughts into your subconscious. Your mind is like an iceberg, that is, the conscious part of your brain is the top 10% and the hidden 90% is your subconscious.

It's also your subconscious that controls 90% of your actions and virtually all of your ideas and attitudes which affect everything else in your life. **In essence, it controls you.**

There are some simple strategies that allow you to access your subconscious. The goal is to input the ideas and attitudes you desire into your mind on a continual basis so that gradually your mindset changes to what you want. These strategies allow you to mold yourself to your heart's desire through your subconscious.

Follow these tips to make lasting changes to your subconscious so you can attract your desires:

Tool #1: Positive Self-Talk

Your mind engages itself in a conversation – or rather monologue – the entire time you're awake. **Since you spend all day talking to yourself, why not tell yourself things you want to hear?** Keep it positive and good benefits will follow.

Congratulate yourself on every success, no matter how small. Each success is a victory and leads you toward your goals. Take every opportunity to celebrate and build your confidence.

When you make a mistake, ask yourself how this helps you. What can you learn or gain from this error? Even mistakes can bring the very life lessons that can catapult you toward your success.

Avoid beating yourself up about anything. This negative self-talk ruins your confidence and breeds discontent and failure. If you hear something negative, stop it in its tracks and turn it into something positive.

Use your self-talk to encourage yourself to act in ways that are in accordance – and not contrary to – your goals.

Tool #2: Affirmations

Affirmations are a form of positive self-talk that affirms the traits in you that you desire. You can replace your negative mindset with positive thoughts and images that guide you toward your goals.

Remember the 3 Ps: Affirmations should be personal, present tense, and positive. Personal means to use the words "I", "me", and "my". Write them in the present tense as if this is a trait you already possess. And, of course, you want them to be positive statements.

Use them every single day. Say your affirmations every morning, every night, and whenever you feel the urge to boost your confidence.

Here are some affirmations you can start with:

- ❖ I take advantage of opportunities that present themselves with swift action.
- ❖ I enjoy meeting new people.
- ❖ I am open to new ideas that can help me reach my goals.
- ❖ I take time to plan my actions and then follow my plan.
- ❖ I make healthy choices about the foods I eat.
- ❖ I enjoy exercising because it makes me look good and feel better.

Tool #3: Prayer and Meditation

Take the time to pray and meditate and visualize living the life you'd love living. Experience it with all your senses and it will draw it to you. This type of spiritual self-reflection will help transform your mindset to be in accordance with your visualization.

A successful mindset combined with an organized plan will complete your bridge to success. All you'll have to do is set forth on your journey. Once you do, you'll find that the more you give, the more you'll receive. Soon enough, you'll truly delight in the life you always desired.

TOOLS-TO-USE NOTES

MIND TOOLS TO CHANGE YOUR LIFE

1. Positive Self-Talk
2. Affirmations
3. Prayer and Meditation

38 STELLA FRANCES

« Chapter Five »

THE CHECKLIST

I HOPE YOU'VE ENJOYED reading "Being Happier. Living The Life You Love." If you're new to these concepts, I encourage you to keep an open mind and give the tools and strategies mentioned in this book a try.

Use the following checklist after you've read the book. Check everything that you're doing right now, then integrate additional action steps – one at a time – into your everyday routine.

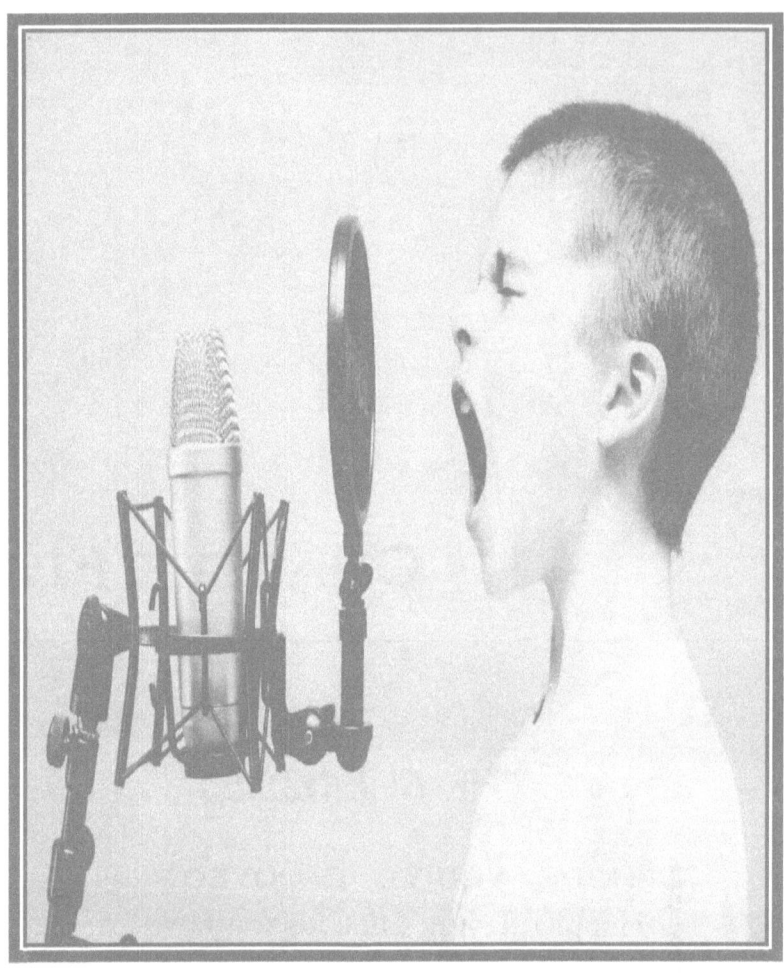

When we are no longer able to change a situation,
we are challenged
to change ourselves.
Viktor E Frankl

Living In The Moment

- ✓ Watch the movie *The Peaceful Warrior*.
- ✓ Take time to stop and smell the roses.
- ✓ Avoid total focus on your goals – enjoy your present life.
- ✓ Make the most of each moment.
    - o Learn from your mistakes.
    - o Look for the silver lining.
- ✓ Eliminate time spent waiting.

Choosing Conscious Living

- ✓ Clarify your principles and live by them.
- ✓ Set priorities in your life and use them to simplify your decisions.
- ✓ Choose an optimistic attitude.
- ✓ Simplify and enrich your lifestyle.
    - o Eliminate clutter from your schedule.
    - o Eliminate clutter from your surroundings.
    - o Spend time with family to strengthen relationships.

Feeling and Showing your Gratitude

- ✓ Tell others when they make you happy.
- ✓ Keep a gratitude journal.
- ✓ Give thanks for your day.

Over-Delivering on your Promises

- ✓ Do I have an abundance mindset?
- ✓ Do I deliver more than expected?

Tools to Change your Life

- ✓ Positive self-talk
  - o Congratulate yourself on your successes.
  - o Avoid beating yourself up about anything.
  - o Find the good in your mistakes.
  - o Encourage your good actions and thoughts.
- ✓ Use affirmations several times a day.
- ✓ Pray or meditate twice daily (in the morning and before bedtime).

Take Action to Live The Life You Love

- ✓ Create an action plan you know you can accomplish with S.M.A.R.T. goals.
    - o Specific
    - o Measurable
    - o Attainable - divide your bigger goals up into small goals
    - o Realistic
    - o Timely
- ✓ Implement your action plan.
    - o Start with easy, quick tasks.
    - o Reward yourself for each accomplishment.
    - o Change your plan if necessary, to ensure success.

When we strive to become better than we are, everything around us becomes better too.

Paulo Coelho

ACT II:

EMPOWERING WORKBOOK

invite more happiness into your life through the practice of self-reflection

46 STELLA FRANCES

« Chapter Six »

BEING HAPPIER THROUGH REFLECTION WORKBOOK

You can either read the guidebook in its entirety and then come back to the workbook, working through the section and refer back to the guidebook for more information as needed. Or if you prefer, you can read a chapter of the guide, and then work through the pages in this workbook. Either method works. Choose the one that works best for you and your style of learning.

Work through the material at your own pace. There is no right or wrong way to start Being Happier. Take your time and really think about what you want in your life. It's important to write things down.

Not only will it help you get very clear about what you want, it also helps deepen your connection with it and gets you well on your way towards manifesting the things you want. It's also nice to be able to look back a few weeks or months from now and notice how much of what you've wanted to change in your life has already changed for the better.

As you read through the ACTI: Guidebook, you'll learn that you have to change your mind at a conscious and subconscious level to change the vibrations you're giving off.

Writing will help you get there sooner. Ideally, grab a pen, get comfortable, turn your phone off, and start working through the short exercises of this workbook. Run out of space? Use extra paper and express yourself. You don't have to work through in one sitting. Take your time, reflect on what you want to accomplish, write it down, and then come back when you're ready to work on the next section.

Let your soul be your guide.

Nothing splendid was ever achieved except by those who dared to believe that something inside them was superior to their circumstances.
Bruce Barton

BEING HAPPIER EXERCISES
Exercise #1

How to focus on what you want and what you already have in order to attract more of it. Knowing what you don't want is the first step in attracting what you really want out of life.

1. Decide what it is that you don't want.

1_____
2_____
3_____

2. Decide what it is you DO want.

1_____
2_____
3_____

As you work through the exercises in the rest of this workbook it is important to have an open mind. The trick is to find a way to turn each and every complaint you have into something you do want.

For example, "I don't want to lose my job" becomes "I am a valuable asset to my company."

You do see how this works, don't you?

Exercise #2

How would you like a little breathing room?

I'm going to walk you through a simple process that will help you become very clear about what you want. As you embark on a journey to learn how to attract the things you deserve out of life, an unusual phenomenon will occur...

Suddenly, you'll have more breathing room in your life. What you genuinely desire will become clearer. You'll also gain the strength to pursue goals that had once seemed impossible. This will happen no matter how old or young you are or what shape your finances and relationships are in before you decided to do something about it.

Breathing room occurs during the very moment you're able to separate yourself from what you're currently experiencing. By the time you follow the specifically designed ideas in this lesson, you'll appreciate the kind of freedom you'll receive.

Breathing room brings clarity and creativity to your relationship with money, your family, your job, and your health. Let's take a closer look...To achieve clarity and balance, you need to get rid of all of your "yeah butt's."

Exercise #2 Continued: Write It Down

Here's something you can do right now... think about something you've wanted for a while. Now ask yourself WHY you don't have it. Take your time and be as specific and detailed as possible.

_____
_____
_____
_____
_____
_____
_____
_____

All those "reasons" are your "yeah butt's." Let's suppose you want to attract a new house, "but" you are putting it off because the timing isn't right, or your credit score is too low, or you don't have a big enough down payment.

You do see where this is going. Right?

You've placed your own restrictions and you've given yourself no breathing room. Listen, this is no joke. If you shine the spotlight on your "yeah butt's" you'll have the most measurable, immediate, and potent results. If you change that, you'll have clarity and ease beyond your wildest dreams.

53 BEING **HAPPIER**

Most folks are as happy as they make up their minds to be.
Abraham Lincoln

Exercise #3

What Would Make You Happier?

Your beliefs, thoughts, and attitudes impact your happiness. Take control of your mind and make it work for you. Control your thoughts and build a life that fills you with enthusiasm.

It's important to define what happiness means to you. Otherwise, you may find yourself chasing someone else's idea of what it takes to be happy. Take the time to think about it.

1. What matters for your own happiness?

_____

_____

_____

_____

2. What would it take to make you happier?

_____

_____

_____

_____

Exercise #4

Write Your Affirmations

Next, it's time to start writing affirmations that can help you change your mindset, eliminate bad habits, create good habits, and attract the life you desire.

Remember, your affirmations should be Positive, Personal (use the word "I", "me", and "my"), and Present Tense (as if you already exhibit that trait).

You can use affirmations in many areas of your life. I've listed some of the areas you may wish to strengthen below:

Your Financial Life – *your career, income, investments, and savings.*

_____
_____
_____
_____

Your Relationships – *with your partner, parents, children, or friends*

_____
_____
_____
_____

Physical – *for eating right, exercising, and good health*

_____

_____

_____

_____

Mental Attitudes – *your success mindset, confidence, and self-esteem*

_____

_____

_____

_____

Your Spiritual Life – *your inner peace, faith, and deeper purpose*

_____

_____

_____

_____

Habits You Want to Break – *addictions like smoking, drinking, over-eating*

_____

_____

_____

_____

Good Habits You Want to Encourage – *like exercise, happiness, and communication*

_____
_____
_____
_____

There is nothing noble in being superior to your fellow man; true nobility is being superior to your former self.
Ernest Hemingway

ACT III:

KEY FACTS

« Chapter Seven »

SECRETS TO LIVING A MEANINGFUL LIFE

THE HUSTLE and bustle of daily life can sweep us away from what really means the most to us. It's up to each of us to figure out how to live a personally fulfilling life. Although much of your life is shared with others, you can still carve out your own space for a rich, meaningful life. Take action now to live a life that you love.

Clarify what matters to you. How you spend your time largely determines what's important to you. If you say your family is at the top of your list, do you spend the bulk of your spare time with them? When you know for sure who and what matters most to you, then that's where you want to focus your time and energy.

Stay in the moment. If you're planting flowers, think about packing the earth well and digging the hole deeply enough. Remind yourself to water them immediately afterward. Regardless of what you're involved in, keep your mind focused.

Even when you're washing the pots and pans, you can concentrate on having nice, hot water and shining the outside of the pans the way you like them.

Say what you mean and mean what you say. Do your words carry importance and honesty, along with kindness and care? Avoid mincing words. Get to the point, but remember to take the other person's feelings into consideration. When your discussions contain subjects of interest and heartfelt feelings, it's meaningful for you and the listener.

Find your passion. What gets you interested, excited, or fascinated? Has there ever been a topic that you think about all day long to the point where you can hardly stand it? If so, follow your passion. Make it an important part of your life as often as you can.

If it's golf, play it as often as you can. If your passion is working with children, then pursue it, whether it's through working at a nursery school, becoming a school teacher, or serving as the neighborhood babysitter. Make it happen.

Worry less about what others think. Pay more attention to what you think. If someone isn't a relevant player in your personal life, then what they believe about you is irrelevant. What you believe about yourself is what matters. Use your emotional fortitude in ways that make your life better. Ensure that your opinion of yourself is great!

Instead of complaining, accept the situation or take action. If what you're upset about is out of your control, it might be time to just accept it. However, if it's something that's within your power to change, take action. Complaining is a waste of your precious time. Focus on problem-solving instead.

Accept responsibility for your life. If you're unhappy, there's no reason to blame your parents, spouse, or boss. Step up and make some decisions to alter what troubles you. You are the captain of your own ship. Figure out the course you want to take and then stay on it.

Refuse to criticize. Focus on assessing your own life instead. Notice the good qualities in others. Making positive changes in yourself is where your power lies.

"Be the change you want to see in the world." Mahatma Gandhi, a great man of peace, first said this quote. Make a difference in your own life and the lives of others. You'll absolutely love yourself for it. Others will love what you're doing, too. Volunteer. Join a club. Get involved!

An enriching life is here for the taking. When your focus is clear, you can then expend your energy on the people and things that matter in your life. Isn't it time to begin the journey toward a life filled with positivity and meaning?

Don't you believe *You* deserve it?

For fast-acting relief, try slowing down.
Lily Tomlin

TIPS TO BE HAPPIER

Have you ever met someone that didn't want more happiness? The pursuit of happiness seems to be an ongoing quest for most people. Luckily, finding happiness might be much easier than you think. Many times, simple solutions can be effective.

Consider these tips to bring more happiness into your life:

1. **Ask for support and be supportive.** Most of us enjoy the feeling of helping others. You can also accomplish a lot more if you simply ask for help and support when you need it.

2. **Make your life simpler.** Having too many tasks, commitments, and physical items in your life makes everything harder. Only keep the commitments, people, and items that you love.

3. **Volunteer.** Helping others and seeing that your life isn't so bad is sure to make you happier.

4. **Take the time to create.** Everyone has a creative genius inside of them, but most of us rarely get to use it. Find a creative project and let your imagination run wild.

5. **Surround yourself with happy people.** It's hard to be happy when those around you are unhappy. Find a few individuals who consistently seem happy and develop new friendships.

6. **Be flexible and open-minded.** If you're inflexible or closed-minded, you're probably miserable. When no one is

living up to your expectations, how can you be happy? The more carefree you can be, the happier you'll be.

7. **Listen to music you love.** Music is a great way to unwind, relax, get excited, and feel motivated. Music can change your emotions, so use it to your advantage.

8. **Sleep enough.** Too little sleep makes you grumpy and is bad for your health. Enjoy better days by getting enough sleep the night before.

9. **Simply do your best.** If you try to do your best, life is much simpler. There's no more deciding how much effort you'll put into something and no regrets that you didn't try hard enough.

10. **Watch less TV.** Perhaps nothing wastes more time than watching TV. It's mostly a way to avoid a boring and unhappy life. Go find something to do that actually makes you happy.

11. **Be well-rounded.** Some of us are great with money, but in horrible physical shape. Others have a great social life, but are at war with their families. Having balance in all aspects of your life makes a big impact. Work on the areas of your life that aren't as strong.

12. **Try new things.** Odds are you haven't played your favorite sport or read your favorite book yet. You might not have even met your best friend yet or tried your favorite food either. You won't find any of these things if you're not open to new possibilities.

13. **Embrace spontaneity.** Planning can be a good thing, but spontaneity has the potential to be great, too.

14. **Exercise each day.** Exercise can boost your mood and help your waistline. Find a form of exercise you truly enjoy.

15. **Spend time on a hobby you love.** Hobbies are things you do because you want to, not because you have to. Finding a hobby is a great way to channel your creative side, while also relaxing and escaping from the stresses of life.

16. **Stop waiting.** There are only so many tomorrows. Get started by doing some of the things you've been putting off until "the time is right."

17. **Read regularly.** Reading can be a healthy distraction and great form of entertainment. It can also teach you things you didn't already know.

18. **Plan an exciting future.** Part of happiness is having something to look forward to. Give yourself a compelling future.

Do you see how simple it can be to increase the level of happiness in your life? Add a few of these items to your life each day and measure the results. Being happy doesn't have to be complicated. Many of the best things in life are simple and free.

If you want to be happy, set a goal that commands your thoughts, liberates your energy, and inspires your hopes.
Andrew Carnegie

NOTES AT A GLANCE

bite size, useful practical information you can put to work for you right-away.

NOTES AT A GLANCE:
Being Happier - The Basics #1

1. Living In The Moment

- ✓ Watch the movie The Peaceful Warrior.
- ✓ Take time to stop and smell the roses.
- ✓ Avoid total focus on your goals – enjoy your present life, too.
- ✓ Make the most of each moment.
- ✓ Learn from your mistakes.
- ✓ Look for the silver lining.
- ✓ Eliminate time spent waiting.
- ✓ Feel exuberance and excitement.

NOTES AT A GLANCE:
Being Happier - The Basics #2

2. Choosing Conscious Living

- ✓ Clarify your principles and live by them.
- ✓ Set priorities in your life and use them to simplify your decisions.
- ✓ Choose an optimistic attitude.
- ✓ Simplify and enrich your lifestyle.
- ✓ Eliminate clutter from your schedule.
- ✓ Eliminate clutter from your surroundings.
- ✓ Eat dinner at home with your family to strengthen your relationships.

NOTES AT A GLANCE:
Being Happier -The Basics #3 & 4

3. Feeling and Showing your Gratitude

- ✓ Tell others when they make you happy.
- ✓ Keep a gratitude journal.
- ✓ Give thanks for your day.

4. Over-Delivering on your Promises

- ✓ Do I have an abundance mindset?
- ✓ Do I deliver more than expected?

NOTES AT A GLANCE:
Being Happier -The Basics #5

5. Mind Tools to Change your Life

- ✓ Positive self-talk
- ✓ Congratulate yourself on your successes.
- ✓ Avoid beating yourself up about anything.
- ✓ Find the good in your mistakes.
- ✓ Encourage your good actions and thoughts.
- ✓ Use affirmations several times a day.
- ✓ Pray or meditate twice daily (in the morning and before bedtime).

NOTES AT A GLANCE:
Being Happier -The Basics #6

6. Take Action to Make your Dreams Come True

- ✓ Create an action plan you know you can accomplish with S.M.A.R.T. goals.
- ✓ Specific
- ✓ Measurable
- ✓ Attainable - divide your bigger goals up into small goals
- ✓ Realistic
- ✓ Timely
- ✓ Implement your action plan.
- ✓ Start with easy, quick tasks.
- ✓ Reward yourself for each accomplishment.
- ✓ Change your plan if necessary, to ensure success.

READ MUCH ABOUT THE SUBJECT

There are many resources on the subject. I encourage you to start learning and answering all the questions you will have after reading this simple introduction to such a complex matter.

Also, check out the short list of books I am including in the Acquiring Knowledge, section at the end of the book and other Stella Note titles that can further help you understand essential elements that contribute to our happiness and ultimately success.

There is good in everything, if only we look for it.
Laura Ingalls Wilder

ACT IV:

Happiness Builders

Tools-To-Use

« Chapter Eight »

The Trouble Tree

I read this story the other day and I wanted to make sure I shared it with you. It helped me keep things into perspective and remember what's important to me.

Here's how it goes: The carpenter I hired to help me restore an old farmhouse had just finished a rough first day on the job. A flat tire made him lose an hour of work, his electric saw quit and now his ancient pickup truck refused to start.

While I drove him home, he sat in stony silence. On arriving he invited me in to meet his family. As we walked toward the front door, he paused briefly at a small tree, touching the tips of the branches with both hands. Upon opening the door he underwent an amazing transformation.

His tan face was wreathed in smiles and he hugged his two small children and gave his wife a kiss.

Afterward he walked me to the car. We passed the tree and my curiosity got the better of me. I asked him about what I had seen him do earlier. "Oh, that's my trouble tree", he replied. " I know I can't help having troubles on the job, but one thing for sure, troubles don't belong in the house with my wife and children.

So I just hang them up on the tree every night when I come home. Then in the morning I pick them up again." "Funny thing is," he smiled, "when I come out in the morning to pick them up, there aren't nearly as many as I remember hanging up the night before."

Find a place to hang your worries, for the most part they will be gone by the time dawn comes.

I believe you can be happier. I believe in you.

Words of Wisdom

wise words spoken by some of
the most powerful and
advanced thinkers in our
world. Listen to the
echo of their voices
and use their wisdom in
your moment-to-moment life.

WORDS OF WISDOM

Stop chasing the money and start chasing the passion." --
TONY HSIEH

WORDS OF WISDOM

Happiness is a butterfly, which when pursued, is always beyond your grasp, but which, if you will sit down quietly, may alight upon you.
Nathaniel Hawthorne

WORDS OF WISDOM

"I owe my success to having listened respectfully to the
very best advice,
and then going away and doing the exact opposite.
G.K. CHESTERTON

Pearls Of Kindness

powerful affirmations to inspire and motivate you

POWERFUL HEARTFELT AFFIRMATIONS

Listening To Music Lifts My Spirits.

I love listening to music! When I am hard at work, my pace becomes attuned to the rhythms of my music. At home, my favorite songs help me to relax. Singing along is fun and makes me feel good.

Singing gives me energy. I feel optimistic and view the world with greater clarity. Dancing has the same effect. Simply moving my body to a rhythm relieves stress.

I may look silly sometimes, but I always feel good inside.

Sometimes, I just listen. The old and familiar tunes of my childhood trigger fond memories. I reminisce as each song brings forth a new wave of nostalgia. Occasionally, I make connections of the present with the past. I discover new avenues to completing objectives.

I like keeping a melody in my head. At work, it may be inappropriate for me to listen to music, so I listen to some music that I really enjoy on the way to work. The chorus or a particular riff tends to stick in my mind, accompanying me throughout the day.

Today, I keep my mind open to many different kinds of music. Regardless of my song choice of the moment, listening to music always uplifts me!

POWERFUL HEARTFELT AFFIRMATIONS

I realize that sometimes I have the option of either being right or being happy.
<u>I choose</u> to be happy.

Life is good. I engage in the kind of work I choose. I relish in opportunities to spend time with the people I love. Each day seems like a new beginning for me

Of course, I realize that my life is less than perfect at times. Yet, even when situations occur that are out of my control, I am truly pleased to be me.

88 STELLA FRANCES

Relaxing Mandalas

Express Your Inner-Artist

beautiful mandalas to help you find inner peace by being in the moment

You can use color pencils or just your regular pen, markers are not recommended as the ink may bleed through the paper.

RELAXING MANDALAS

Whether you're feeling overwhelmed, scattered, or just plain stressed, coloring offers a peaceful and therapeutic way to refocus and reinvigorate your mind.

This form of meditation is becoming increasingly popular as we realize stress isn't something we can just "power through". Meditative practices soothe mind chatter, allowing our inner voice to shine through.

The ritual of mandala coloring moves us into a contemplative state, encouraging us to slow down. Allow your stress to melt away as you enter the world of circles and patterns.

The word Mandala (pronunciation mon- dah- lah) means "circle" and represents the universe in Indian religions. The mandala encompasses friends, family, and communities.

The mandala teaches us life is circular. Life is never-ending. Each moment is another colorful thread in the continually growing tapestry of the universe.

Become one with the Universe as you lose yourself to the flow of lines and color. Allow yourself to move from the doing to the being as you enjoy the process of transformative ritual!

RELAXING MANDALAS

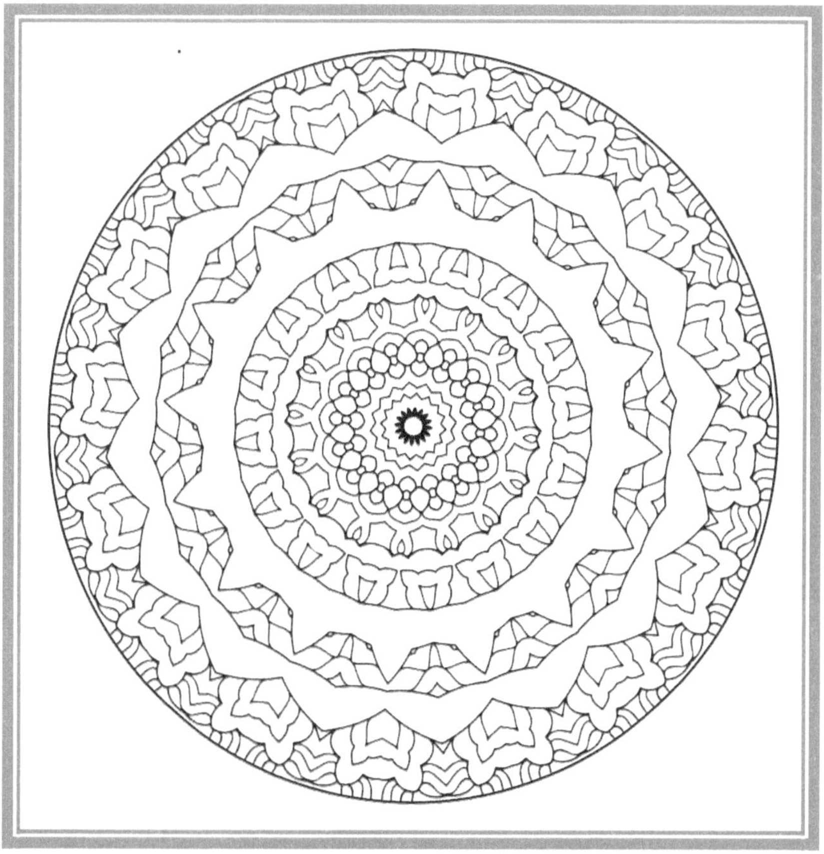

RELAXING MANDALAS

RELAXING MANDALAS

94 STELLA FRANCES

IN CLOSING

BONUS MATERIAL

A Gift For You

POWERFUL HEARTFELT AFFIRMATIONS

The Road To Happiness Is As Long Or Short As I Make It To Be.

I envision the path to happiness as a road through the desert, in July. The heat radiates off the asphalt, so I am unsure of just how far the road stretches off into the distance. Of course, this is my vision, so the road is as long—or short—as I want it to be.

With my mind, I create oases and mountains that provide shade. **I create the happiness.**

I am in control of my happiness, because happiness is perceived. **Happiness is a goal always within grasp, though many perceive it to be at the end of the road.** *However, I avoid waiting for the end of the road. I place happiness among my belongings and carry it with me during my travels.*

By maintaining a positive outlook, searching for the good in things, and reinforcing my well-being, my happiness grows within. I begin to feel optimistic. I discover that happiness affects my recognition of success.

When I am happy, I succeed in every challenge I undertake. **Life is easier, people are nicer, and each obstacle appears smaller.**

Today, I intend to share my perspective on happiness with others. Instead of being a goal to work toward, **I realize that happiness is actually a tool I can use to achieve my goals.** *I have stopped striving to be happy.* **I simply am.**

Self-Reflection Questions:

1. What helps me to maintain a positive mental outlook?
2. What type(s) of happiness does success bring?
3. Who and/or what influences my well-being?

Voice your thoughts here…

_____
_____
_____
_____
_____
_____
_____
_____
_____
_____

AFTERWORD

resource guide for living a better, happier purpose-driven life

★ ♥ ☀

A NOTE FROM STELLA FRANCES

If you've made it this far, then I can tell we are going to be friends. You - like me - are always exploring how you can grow and be your best-self. I'm inspired by people like you and would love to embrace you as part of the tribe.

To learn more about how to *"Find Your Happy"* by creating a meaningful and purpose driven life visit StellaFrances.com or come to a private workshop or mini-retreat where we can meet in person and we can dig into Careers & Relationships over soulful conversations. For a list of upcoming events remember to go to: StellaFrances.com/events/

I'd love to connect with you and hear about your journey. So be sure to stay in touch. Feel free to send me a quick note or say hello on Facebook and keep me posted. I'm here to help.

Here's to leading a life of purpose and living with passion.

Stella xo

PS Visit the blog StellaFrances.com/blog page for daily inspiration and tips on creating the life you love living. I can help you succeed in your pursuit of happiness.

PPS As, Zig Ziglar once said... "*People often say that motivation doesn't last. Well, neither does bathing, that's why we recommend it daily"*

A SPECIAL INVITATION
Find Your Happy Discovery Call

Set up An Exclusive Appointment with A Whole New Level Of Happiness.

Are you ready to move your happiness up to a new level?

Explore and Discover What Really Matters To You. I invite you to a complimentary call with me to explore and discover the ways to bring more happiness into your life.

We all experience the ups and downs of life and I'm here to help keep you going in the right direction, just because we all deserve to be happy.

A "Find-Your-Happy" Discovery Session is a 30-minute call. where we talk about where in life you are now and where you'd love to be.

Specifically, here's what we will cover during our call:

<u>The 3 D's:</u>

1. *Discover* the longing and discontent in the areas of your life you'd like to improve and what is costing you to stay where you are. That would be our first step.

2. *Design* a clear vision for the quality of life you desire and what's worth to take happiness to the next level. That would be our second step.

3. ***Decide*** to take today the action that will move you from where you are to where you want to be. That would be the third step in taking your Happiness to a higher level.

Leave this session feeling uplifted and inspired knowing that you have the power to change your life and that the power within you is far greater than your current life conditions and circumstances.

Right now, you're standing at the doorway to your new ideal life. Get clear on exactly where you are, what you'd like to create, and the next most important step you can take that will move you in the direction of a happier-purpose driven life.

Join me for a complimentary 30-min. discovery call. Every week I make sure I carve out a chunk of time to offer free service to community. This is my way to say thank you and "pay-it-forward." As you can imaging spots are limited. To schedule your session, jump over to the website and let's talk soon. To access my calendar, go to StellaFrances.com/calendar/

I'm here to help.

YOUR NEXT BEST STEP
Need More In-Depth Guidance Creating A Happiness Based Life?

These will help...

We have created some incredibly in-depth programs, courses and products to help you every step of the way on your pursuit of happiness. And as with everything we do at Elevated Awareness, they come with a 100% results-backed guarantee. That's just how confident I am they work.

Two great places to start are:

An Empowering Self-Discovery Adventure

Find Your Happy

Find it and Claim it. Know who you are and be who you are. With this step-by-step framework Stella helps her clients take time to find themselves, understand what they want in their lives, and take effective right action to make their dreams come true. This program is for you if you want to bring more happiness and success into your life by finding meaning, purpose and direction.

Happiness fuels success; **if you want to be more successful, be happier.** Stella's coaching will empower you to achieve your goals whilst simultaneously increasing your happiness. Take action and begin your pursuit of true happiness, today.

A Journey Into Life Mastery

THE PASSPORT

Passport to your dream. If you are ready for a new destination. If it feels like something is missing where you are in your life right now, get ready to DEFINE your IDEAL outcome and DECIDE to go after it.

If you're willing to commit to your happiness and ready to take action to change your life, then you have found the program that will help you move forward.

THE PASSPORT is a step-by-step proven system that helps you get crystal clear on what you want and gives you the tools and strategies to stay true to yourself. Learn the simple steps that will take you from wherever you are now (stuck, frustrated, scared, unhappy) to confident and fulfilled as you learn exactly how to define your dream and develop a concrete plan to achieve it.

When you are in harmony with your soul's purpose and with what you are here to be and do, things get easier. This is the most passionate, wondrous way to live life. Sign up and start living the life you were meant to live.

VIP Day Every intensive is unique. You may choose to come work with me in person, or virtually from the comfort of your own home or office. Join me for jam-packed self-discovery action over the course of a fun filled day.

STELLA NOTES & CLUB ★ HAPPY

Solutions From The Soul

Winning ways to play the game of life. Check out this popular mini guide series on finding true lasting happiness and take your life to the next level. Stella Notes are short writings super loaded with practical tools, easy-to-use strategies, and pearls of wisdom to help you uncover your passions, remove roadblocks and get you moving from where you are to where you want to be.

Imagine what it would feel like to belong to a group that combined the benefits of a social group, mastermind group, support group, cheerleader group. Imagine what it would feel like to create relationships with like-minded people who not only understand your thirst to discover your truth and make your dreams come true, but who also believe that you can achieve the goals you set for yourself.

These are just some of the benefits you will enjoy as a member of Club-Happy. Visit StellaFrances.com/clubhappy

Curious to know more? All of the courses, products and free resources to support you on your life journey can be found at: StellaFrances.com

Make your journey a fun one.

"Success Begins with Happiness"
Stella Frances

About Stella Frances

Mentor, Coach, Speaker, Creator of Stella-Notes

Stella Frances, founder of Elevated Awareness, inspires and empowers all those that are drawn to her to live their highest vision in the context of love and joy.

As a Success Principles, Jack Canfield Certified Trainer and as a Mary Morrissey Certified DreamBuilder Coach, Stella can help you design and manifest a life that's in harmony with your soul's purpose.

After 15 successful years in the I.T. industry, Stella-Frances found herself more passionate in coaching her clients around systems for life than in I.T. systems. Her passion is teaching clients discover & unlock their unique potential, find true happiness and achieve success to live a life they LOVE living.

Stella is an inspiring speaker, passionate educator, and a highly sought-after happiness coach.

What is the biggest challenge you're facing right now? And what would you love to create? Let Stella help you, or your employees break through the obstacles that are holding you back. You will be glad you did.

To contact Stella, go to her website at StellaFrances.com

Qualifications and Certifications
- Success Principles Trainer - Jack Canfield (Chicken Soup for the Soul)
- DreamBuilder Coach - Mary Morrissey, Transformational Coaching
- Access Bars™ Practitioner & Facilitator, Access Consciousness
- Langevin Certified Instructor/Facilitator

Programs and Workshops

Stella Frances gives talks and leads workshops all over the United States and the Caribbean Islands.

She also conducts retreats, intensives, and training programs.

To learn more, go to StellaFrances.Com/Events

Island Retreat with Stella Frances
The Voyage

ADVENTURES INTO HAPPINESS

The ticket to happiness is hidden in your heart. Get out of your day-to-day grind and jump into the source of authentic happiness. Connect with nature as you set your intentions to bring more happiness into your life.

Create a powerful vision of your IDEAL life, set goals and define effective action to make it happen. Learn how to change your thoughts to change your world.

If you'd like Stella's personal help in defining the framework and start building an exciting life based on your definition of happiness, these small-group private retreats held in exclusive locations like the quaint Bahamas, Jamaica, and Jupiter Beach offer a tranquil, transformational environment and personalized support you need to awaken to the best <u>You</u>.

Reject stress and give yourself the gift of time to attain inner-peace and a sense of empowerment. Get inspired with our sunrise meditation on the beach. Enjoy healthy delicious freshly cooked meals. Come home with an island mindset and a solid plan to maintain it, no matter how gray the sky gets.

Recharge and Reboot At A Retreat By-The-Sea.

For information and to reserve your spot, contact Stella at Happier@StellaFrances.com

Bring The Power Of Change To Your Organization

Steps to Success

KEYNOTE, WORKSHOP, AND TRAINING

Positive change and profound success are the results when your employees and managers, experience **Steps to Success** in a live group workshop, training, or keynote.

Not only will your team be inspired and motivated to achieve greater success, but they'll also learn how to up-level all their mind-sets, actions, relationships, and strategic alliances.

Steps to Success Keynote, Workshop, or Training will empower them with strategies that make them more productive, help put more money in their paychecks, help them function better within their workgroups, and respond more effectively and productively to everyday events.

The **Steps to Success** is ideal for groups such as:
- ❖ Small-business owners
- ❖ Managers and executives
- ❖ Corporate workgroups and new hires
- ❖ Professional practitioners and their staffs
- ❖ Work-at-home employees and telecommuters
- ❖ Employees facing layoff or transfer

To learn more, go to StellaFrances.com or contact Stella at Happier@StellaFrances.com

90-Day Programs with Stella Frances

The Passport

Voyage into Happiness

A Life Mastery Course of Action. Getting you from where you are to where you want to be.

Find *Your* Happy

A Self-Discovery & Empowerment Journey

Bring more happiness into your life by finding meaning, purpose and direction.

The Ticket
You Were Born To Be Happy

A 2-STEP FORMULA TO BRING MORE HAPPINESS & SUCCESS INTO YOUR PROFESSIONAL LIFE
Step 1:   Making your business more effective.
Step 2:   Becoming a more effective *you.*

The Dream Builder
Journey into The Spirit
The Spiritual Laws of Success

Learn how everything is created twice – and how you can use that truth to build your dreams effortlessly.

Stella Frances
YOUR HAPPINESS COACH
GROUP. ONE-ON-ONE. VIP-DAY. RETREATS. WORKSHOPS

Weekend Workshops with Stella

THE MECHANICS OF LIFE

Elevating Self-Awareness

**An Irresistibly Fun Series Of
5 Self-Growth Mix-&-Match Workshops**

#1. Master the Mindset of Success.
#2. Goal Setting For Growth.
#3. Building Inner Confidence.
#4. The Power Of Saying No.
#5. Elevate Your Energy.

The Vision
Tailor Life to Your Dreams

Start actively pursuing the dream that will give you the joy, confidence and happiness you're longing for.

To learn more, go to StellaFrances.com or contact Stella at Happier@StellaFrances.com

Stella Frances
YOUR HAPPINESS COACH
GROUP. ONE-ON-ONE. VIP-DAY. RETREATS. WORKSHOPS

Aquiring Knowledge And Additional Resources For Happiness And Success

I trust you enjoyed reading this Stella Notes book and have found it both helpful and interesting. Above all I hope it piqued your curiosity enough to make you want to dive deeper and learn more.

I suggest and recommend that you read something educational and motivational every day, at least 15-minutes a day, or more. Create a new ritual to inspire and motivate yourself.

Keep reading, keep learning, and keep practicing as you work your way towards the life of your dreams. Happiness is attainable by each one of us. Make it happen.

Knowledge is Power

Also Available In The Stella Notes Series

1. In The Sea of Love
2. Law of Attraction
3. Imagine
4. Dreams Come True
5. Being Happier
6. Inspired
7. No Worries
8. Happy by Habit
9. Mindfully Yours
10. Stuck No More
11. Love ThySelf

Take Your Happiness To The Next Level... Download The FREE Happiness Tools

At StellaFrances.com/resources

Tool #1: Daily Gratitude Journal

Use the Gratitude Journal to record you wins and gifts of the day. It's an awesome self-discovery tool that can help you connect with your unique character strengths.

Tool #2: Stuck? Unstick Yourself Now Worksheet

An easy tool to use for when you feel stuck or want to generate new ideas for a project or goal. This super-effective brainstorming tool helps you come up with lots of new ideas and choose 3 actions to move forward with.

Tool #3: Stressed? Overwhelmed? Speedy Priority Finder

Sometimes your day-to-day priorities differ from your life's priorities. Use this tool to feel more in control and less overwhelmed. Clarify a path to set and realize top priorities.

Tool #4: Daily Success Habits Exercise

By making small changes to your daily routine you can make BIG changes in your life and career. Define 5 new success habits, to help you be more effective.

5-DAY SELF-DISCOVERY COURSE

In this powerful FREE **Grow-Expand-Thrive** mini course -delivered to your email address- you will learn winning ways to find your happy and start living a more fulfilled and meaningful life. Register today at StellaFrances.com

www.ingramcontent.com/pod-product-compliance
Lightning Source LLC
Chambersburg PA
CBHW022106160426
43198CB00008B/370